RADICAL CURIOSITY